A Purpose in Your Pain

By: Lekendra Kemp

ISBN 978-0-578-65407-2

Instagram: @authorlekendra or @blackandhealed

Website: www.blackandhealed.com
Nashville, TN

Dedication

I dedicate this book to the three most important people in my life. My beautiful daughters Aviona and Jaidyn. I love you more than words could ever describe. My prayer is that you both become and do better than me, and live life whole, healed, and with dignity. To my Mother Tina. Thank you for being a great example for me over the years. I have so much respect and admiration for you. I love you!

In loving memory of Howell "Hoss" Atkins

Table of Contents

Introduction

Difficult roads often lead to beautiful destinations. Never regret a day in your life. Good days give you happiness. While bad days give you experiences. Life, no matter how much we try to plan it. Never ends up exactly how we want it to. As kids, some of us dreamed of being rich and famous, married with children, or even to become teachers, doctors, lawyers, or professional athletes. The problem with having plans is that we put limits on what God can do. There is a quote that says, “Man's plans, Gods laughs”. This quote resonates with me and tells me that no matter how great of a plan we set aside for ourselves. We never know where life will take us or even if that is the direction God has set out for us to begin with.

I have had to learn that the hard way. One of the hardest things I have had to learn was allowing myself to fully stop being a control freak over my life and start living in the moment. Really allowing myself to be ok with taking life for what it is and accepting what it isn’t. Not focusing so much on what my expectations on my life should be but focusing more on what was it that God created me to do on this earth. I feel deeply in my heart that if we aren’t living and doing the works that God has set out for us. Using the gifts and talents he has blessed us with. Then we aren’t experiencing what life really is. I had to learn how to be ok when God says “No, not now.” or “No, that’s not the plan I have for you.” I mean let’s keep it real. Most of us only turn to God when we need him anyway. So, by doing that we never take time out to even consult God with what our ideas are to begin with. Let alone to ask Him what plans he has for us and to direct us in the path he has set out for us. I had to learn that God loves an obedient server. He likes to feel wanted and appreciated just like we do.

Today, especially with the craze of social media. Sometimes we must take a minute and completely detox ourselves from it. Social media has a way of placing unrealistic expectations on our lives. Besides, how many people do you see on your timeline openly sharing everything that is wrong with them and their life? Exactly! More than likely never. That’s because people can go on these free apps and create the life they want. People share what they want you to know. Whether it be lies, truth, or exaggeration. Comparing our lives to others is easy when we have access to photos and posts from people who seem to be doing more and better than you. Everyone is an entrepreneur now, everyone is announcing engagements, posting wedding pictures, graduating from college, and traveling the world. Yet, you might be at a season of your life where you don't even know how your rent will be getting paid this month. What you're going to eat for dinner. Or even if you want to live to see the next day. I have been there, and a few times.

We sometimes are so busy planning our lives that we forget to live it. With doing that we often take things for granted. Neglecting ourselves mentally, physically, and spiritually and completely losing sight of who we are and what we are called by God to do. God did not place any of us on this earth to fail. God never told us life would be easy.

The greatest accomplishment any of us can have is knowing our true purpose on Earth. God has created us all in His image. We are all made to do something specific on this earth. We all have a purpose. No matter how big or small that is. We all aren't called to do the same things. That's just reality. The great thing about that is once we learn what our purpose is, we will begin to live in our truth. Live real and fulfilled lives. Learn the true meaning of what happiness really is and what it looks and feels like for you. We won't be so conformed with trying to compete to society's standards of how our lives should be, but be authentic, and genuinely happy with who we are and without approval of others.

I believe that once you become a certain age or maybe even go through a certain experience. You will start appreciating life more and learn to take things more seriously. You will have life changing events that will happen to you in your life that will force you to have to check yourself. A moment where you start analyzing your life and really thinking about if you are living up to God's expectations for your life. Or are you just doing whatever it is you want to do and being complacent? Ask yourself, are you living or just existing?

In the workplace it is often said that we should want to work "smarter, not harder". This can be applied to life as well. There is no need for any of us to be putting time and effort chasing after things we were never called to do. Chasing after people God never intended to be in our lives to begin with. Time is not on our side. It is imperative that we not only take life seriously but to not live in regret. So, whatever it is that is holding you back. Release it! Let it go! We were not placed on this earth to live or lead with fear, but by love.

Chapter 1: Childhood

I would say that growing up I had more good times than bad. I am so thankful to be raised by such a strong, hardworking, caring, and dedicated woman like my Mom. I grew up in a very small town called Franklin, KY as an only child. As a kid living in Franklin, I hated it. I always had big city dreams. I honestly didn't grow to appreciate my hometown until I started having kids of my own and I realized how great of a family town it really is. Everyone knows everybody, and of the black population I am related to about 90 % of the black people in the town.

I would split my time between my Mom in Kentucky and my Dad in Mississippi. I swear that man has lived all over the state. Before I was old enough to start school, I would spend a lot of time in Starkville, MS. As I got older, we moved around to Kosciusko, Weir, Ackerman, and Tupelo, Mississippi with my Dad. I hated Mississippi as a kid. It was so country and so boring. My Dad and his family grew up in low income housing. As an adult now I would say that Brookville Garden Apartments in Starkville, MS is hands down the worst projects I have ever seen and experienced. I spent most of my childhood there with my Dad because that's where my grandparents lived.

I remember summers there being in the free food program. We would go to the center or school by the projects and wait for them to pass us a sack lunch. Then walk back home. Something bad was always going on. A fight, somebody getting shot, drugs, etc. My Daddy did not play. I couldn't do anything. I had to stay in the house or right on the sidewalk where I could be seen. I couldn't play with any of the other kids because he always said they were too grown acting. I couldn't go to the community pool or playground either. The only fun I ever had was when my cousins came around.

My Dad became even more strict once he became a Pastor. I would go to Mississippi every summer once I started school. The towns my Daddy lived in didn't even have paved roads. They were either roads made with red clay dirt or gravel. Weir, MS was the town my Dad eventually moved to when I was about 11 years old. This town had one school, one grocery store called the Sunflower, a post office, and a library. That's it.

I couldn't watch tv unless it was something my Dad approved. I couldn't listen to music unless it was gospel. On Sunday's I had to wear dresses with slips and put pretty hair bows in my hair. I say till this day that he is the reason

I hate wearing dresses now. We were at church at least 6 times out of the 7 days of the week. We raised animals. I could go to my Dad's backyard and find horses, pigs, chickens, cows, dogs, and sometimes deer. I had a horse named Lady who I loved so much. This is where I began my love and appreciation for nature. I couldn't do much so I would sit outside in those big country fields and just imagine what life was like in the city. When my Mom would call to check on me, I would ask her to put the phone up to some music so I could hear something besides gospel for just a few minutes. Every time I would ask her to, she would crack up laughing but she would always do it for me. My Dad was very overprotective and sometimes controlling. Once I turned 12, I asked my Mom if I could make the decision on if I had to go down there for the summer. She allowed me to choose and I never spent another summer there again.

Living most of my life with my Mom I didn't grow up poor, but I didn't grow up rich either. I remember being raised in the projects, or what us locals call the APT, short for apartments of course. We lived in A building. I had a best friend who lived in the apartment right behind me, Cameron Jackson. He was like the little brother I always wanted. Annoying at times. We argued often, but we always were there for one another. Till this day no matter how long we go not seeing or speaking to each other. He is one person I know I can trust and genuinely loves and respects me. I remember spending a lot of time there and at other family members' houses. Especially my Aunt Sissy's house. She lived in J building with my two cousins Latoya and Brastin. Brastin was hardly ever home. When he was he was being overprotective over Toya and I per usual. Or somewhere rapping and dancing. I know I had to get on Toya's nerves. Everywhere she went I wanted to go. Everything she did I wanted to do. I always looked up to her. She was always the "cool girl" to me. I wanted to dress like her and even hang with her friends. Brastin was the big brother I always wanted. He always had my back and I have always had his.

When my Mom went to work, I would go over a friend of the family's house Mrs. Francis house she also lived in the APT. They loved me and treated me like their own. I loved going over there. I would ride my big wheel around the roundabout. Or go play in the area with the trees beside Mrs. Mae's house and climb trees all day. Or wait for Mr. Beasley to pull up in his truck so I could get me some cheese popcorn or a Tweety Bird popsicle. I loved the bubble gum eyes in that popsicle. One of my most memorable moments staying over Mrs. Francis house was with a man named James. He was like an uncle to me. I remember I was peeing on myself. I had to be like 4 years old and how I remember this till this day I have no idea. Well, I guess he had enough of me having accidents. So, one day he told me "Lekendra if you pee on yourself, I am going to put you in the oven and cook you." I was terrified. I never used the bathroom on myself again. I still laugh about that.

When I got old enough to go to school, I stayed with two of Mom's friends while she went to work. One was Vicky, who I call Aunt Vicky. I loved staying with her. She was always so fun. She would braid my hair, take me shopping and to get my nails done. She always had a spotless home. Reminded me a lot of my Mom. I believe they both have OCD. The other was Sheila. I loved staying there too because she was also a hairdresser. So, she would babysit me, and I could get my hair done at the same time. Plus, she was always cooking something or baking something. She is the reason why still till this day I love chocolate chess cake. She makes the best I have ever had.

I don't know how my Mom managed to raise me as well as she did. A single Mother, never married, never owned a car, never even learned how to drive. No fancy college degrees, and no fancy jobs either. She worked hard to give me any and everything I ever wanted. I know there were times when things got hard. Especially once we left the APT and moved to Breckenridge Street in a black neighborhood called Newtown. When we first left the projects, Mom was still on welfare and food stamps, and she babysat on the side. Which I loved because it gave me a chance to play with other kids. Even though I was very content with playing by myself, and I still enjoy my alone time versus being around a group till this day. I can say that I have plenty of childhood friends that stood in the gap of me not having siblings.

Being an only child had its good moments and its bad moments for sure. There were some days I could see the frustration on my Mom's face, but she never vocally told me her struggles. She always kept it in. Which she still does today, and it drives me crazy. With her doing that she would sometimes take it out on me. I would go from being a kid to an adult and dealing with having to hear her vent to me with things I wasn't even old enough to understand. Which turned our relationship more of a best friend role instead of a Mother daughter role in my opinion. The only real memories I have of us struggling is sometimes our heater wouldn't work in the winter. It was one of those heaters with the pilot lights. I remember we would have to press, and press, and press on this button to get the flame to ignite and some days it just wouldn't. So, we would have to heat the house with the stove. Or days where she needed money for food, but we had used all the stamps for the month so she would send me to the Food Lion with rolled change. I would ride my bike to the grocery store and buy whatever it is she had written down on the list. Since we didn't have a car, my bike was our transportation when we didn't have a ride. Cruising down the street with bags on both sides of the handlebars and some on my shoulders.

I did typical things as a kid. I danced and loved cheerleading. I was also in drama, chorus, and many other school clubs and activities. I made good grades and I would consider myself to be popular amongst my classmates because I was very active in school. I was always participating in something and I have always been a leader. I don't remember getting in trouble a lot at home. She taught me at an early age how to clean, cook, balance a checkbook, pay bills, grocery shop, do laundry, and how to be an overall good woman. She taught me how to take up for myself when I would get bullied for not being more like the black girls. She supported me and has always been the first person I call when I need anything because she has always been dependable.

In middle school I believe is where I realized I was different from a lot of kids. I remember being in school one day and being so bored that in Social Studies they always taught us the same things. I was over it. So, my best friend at the time and myself decided we were going to ask the only black teacher in the school who also happened to teach Social Studies, Mrs. Moffit how she felt about having African American studies as an option for students to select. She agreed to teach but she told us it had to be approved by the principal. So, we went around school getting autographs for a petition to present to our principal Mr. Hall. We argued back and forth with Mr. Hall. I wasn't taking no for an answer and neither was she. We left that office with exactly what we wanted. Next week we had our African American studies class.

High School were some of the best years of my life. The summer before my 9th grade year I had become close with a girl from school named Kesha. She is currently still my best friend till this day. We were thicker than thieves. If you saw her you saw me. We formed a clique at school called TR short for "The Realest". I laugh now because this was slick a gang. We had t-shirts, a hand sign and everything. We were all best friends in high school. Always into something. Always going somewhere. They were some not so good memories of high school as well. My classmate and friend OJ passed away our sophomore year from a car accident. The day he passed away October 6th ended up being the exact same day my oldest daughter was born.

I would say for the most part I had a very great upbringing, but like every person, my childhood had some memories I am not that fond of. Some memories I would say were the start and the beginning of my first experience with pain and how to cope with pain.

Chapter 2: Pain

Pain is the birth of maturation. It is inevitable and a vital part of growth. None of us will ever escape pain, but we all will deal with pain differently. Pain is a very important step to finding your purpose. Without pain you are unable to feel, and if you are unable to feel then you will be unable to know what it is you need to change. Pain can have a real effect on people. It changes people. It makes you become cautious and guarded unconsciously. Pain causes you not to trust and to spend most of your time overthinking instead of just living.

I think for me and my life the first experience I ever dealt with and the biggest secret I have kept for years was being molested by a family member. I kept this a secret to myself and didn't tell anyone until I began writing this book. I knew that once this book came out and my Mom found out about it. It would hurt her deeply to know that I kept that hidden from her for so long. So, one day I just called her up and told her what had happened and that I was going to be talking about it in my book.

I remember the day it happened very vividly. I had to be about 9 or 10. It was daylight outside. One of my parents had to work that day so I was dropped off to a family member's house to baby sit me. I had never really stayed at this family members house before without my parents. Usually when we came over my parents were with me and we would visit and leave. Somehow the adult that was supposed to watch me had left. I remember sitting in the living room and watching tv and being asked by a male family member to come in a room with him. I remember the size of the room, how the furniture was placed. The sheets on the bed and how he had the TV Guide channel playing on the TV screen.

After he molested me, he went on about his day like nothing happened and told me not to tell anyone that happened because I would get in trouble because they would think I was fast. I remember being so scared and so ready to leave. I was confused, hurt, embarrassed and I initially felt like it was something that I did to cause this. Did I look older than I was? Was I acting “grown”? As often heard in the black community. That was the first time I let a man's words manipulate me. Not knowing I would put myself through that for years with men in my adulthood. From that day forward, I never interacted with that family member. I never spoke to him, never wanted to be or come around him. Still till this day I have no respect for him. I don’t allow my kids around him either.

From that experience of hurt from a man, came another and that was with my relationship with my Dad. Many times, he left me disappointed to where I would literally cry myself to sleep. I never could understand how a person who helps bring a child in this world can neglect their child's emotional and financial needs but be willing to do that consistently for kids that don't even belong to you. Especially when you only have one biological child on this earth. I mean shouldn't your focus be on your child first before you start providing and taking care of another woman's child. A woman who already had five other kids before you at that. I always held that pain inside. Always finding myself wondering what I have done that would keep him from me.

The last time I saw my father face to face was about 4 years ago and I asked him why he wasn't around more. The answers he gave me didn't sit well with me or make me feel any differently than when I hadn't asked him. Instead of taking accountability, owning his part and just apologizing. He decides to play victim and blame it on my Mom. Telling me that my Mom's behavior played a part of him not coming around. As a Mom myself and a single Mom. I don't care what my daughters Fathers do to hurt me. I will never not allow my kids to have a relationship with their Dads. I never felt in my heart that my Mom was doing that. I can count on one hand how many times she called and asked that man for anything. On the other hand. As a Mom, I couldn't go to sleep every night not knowing for myself how my daughters were. Where they lived? How they were being treated? Who and what they were around? Or to live my life knowing I had no input on how they were being raised.

I still remember every promise that was made and not kept. What hurts the most is that he attempted to do the same thing to my oldest daughter. So, I had to nip that in the bud quickly. As of today, he hasn't seen my youngest daughter in person ever and hasn't seen my oldest daughter since she was about 7 or 8. She is 12 years old currently. I can't remember a Christmas or birthday gift that I or my kids have ever received from him. I know it's not about gifts but some years we didn't even receive a phone call. Or when he would call, he wouldn't even know how old I was or how old my kids were.

As an adult I started seeing how the pain I was carrying about my father was spilling over to the relationships I was putting myself in. In relationships I would be emotionally needy and cling to the man who told me everything I wanted to hear and failed to hold them accountable for what they were showing me. Which is the exact way that I treated my father. I felt like the best way to cope with the pain would be to just distance myself. So, I went 4 and a half years without speaking to him. I felt like I had reached a point where it was no longer my job to force a relationship with him. Let alone basic communication. It should never be the child's place to reach out to an adult. I would cry some nights thinking "Does he not even care if I'm alive? How does he know I am not being mistreated, going without food, shelter, or clothes?" To just allow another person to take sole responsibility of a child you helped create and assume everything is fine is not okay.

I am sure growing up without a Father is hard for any child, but a Father who is a man of God makes it even more difficult. I saw myself questioning God. So bad that I stopped believing in God, the church, and religion in general at one point. I would think "How could a man who teaches others about God, family, and being an overall good person neglect the one job he had which is to be a Father?" He made me feel like not only was he a hypocrite but so was God. Like, how could God allow this to even be my life. How could God allow him to get away with this? How could his wife live her life with a man she knows has nothing to do with his own child? At this point the pain was turning into anger and I was taking it out and being mad at everyone. I mean because that is always easy to do. Play victim and blame others for how you feel. Until I learned that the pain you feel is truly that. Only you will feel it. It has no effect on the other person. That's why it's easy for the person that caused you pain to go on with their life freely without any remorse. It's imperative with dealing with pain that we learn and understand the importance of controlling your feelings. We cannot suffocate on the pain that it is causing us. But the real work is not only finding the source of the pain but allowing yourself to realize and have the mental maturity to know that pain is always temporary. There is always a deeper lesson to learn with pain.

Chapter 3: Betrayal

Betrayal never comes from your enemies. It always comes from the people you love the most. When someone betrays you, it reflects their character. It never has anything to do with you. One of the biggest lessons I've learned from betrayal is that it is the only truth about a person that sticks. The biggest form of betrayal I ever experienced would have to be when it comes to my relationships with men. As women we often feel that if we are loyal to a man that he will be loyal to us. That is far from the truth.

I made probably the worst decision I could have ever made in my life by marrying the first man I really loved after high school at 19 years old. At 19 I found myself married, even though my gut instinct told me not to do it. Pregnant with my first child two months later and giving birth to my oldest daughter Aviona at 20 years old. We got married in Warren County, Kentucky courthouse on Valentine's Day in 2007. We argued the day before we went to the courthouse, the day we left the courthouse we argued, and the day we had our license signed we argued.

I was young and so naive. I look back at that girl and all I see is a lost soul. Someone who truly didn't know how to love or receive love. I think back to what my type was then and what I found attractive in a man and the only thing that comes to mine is young and dumb. I was into the thugs. For some reason the bad boys gave me a thrill. I knew my ex-husband was a street guy and I knew what he did in the streets, but I didn't know how deep the streets had him until we took a trip down to Laurel, MS. A city he ran off too when he was 16 years old to join the Rollin 60s Crip gang.

After hours of driving we finally made it late that night. We pulled up to his friend Hands house. (RIP to him he passed away a few years ago from a car accident) When we got out the car it was two guys sitting on the porch. They began telling me all the gang stories. They told me all the things my husband had done to get ranked as an OG in the gang. I knew then I had got myself in some deep shit. I had married not just a typical street dude but a man heavily affiliated with gang life and culture. The next day we went over to another friend's house named T Bone. The plan was for all the members of the gang to come over and have a barbecue. The day quickly turned for the worst. Another set of Crips in the area got word that my husband was in town. Apparently, the reason he left Jackson, TN (his hometown) and Laurel, MS was over some beef with one of their members. The rival gang ended up in front of the house.

They pulled up fast in three to four box Chevy's into the yard. Got out and all I saw was about 20 men fighting. People from my husband's gang were running out of the house. It was people coming from everywhere. A neighbor saw what was happening and called the police.

I was in the house and hid in a room cause. One of the guys came to the door and said "You don't ever have to hide. As long as you are with Cat Daddy you will always be protected." Cat Daddy was the name the gang gave my husband. When the police finally arrived, they started putting everyone in handcuffs who were outside. Well everyone who was left because once they heard the sirens, they cut out quickly. Of course, one of the guys they arrested was my stupid husband. Who was still fighting! I was pissed! I am in a city where I know nobody. Now I am alone, and his ass done got locked up. After being locked up for about 2 hours a bail bondsman finally let him out. After I went down and paid the money to release him. I made him leave to go back to Kentucky right then.

Dating someone heavy in the streets is hard. I felt I could change him to make him want to be a better person. I felt like if I wanted more for his life he should too. I was so intrigued by his bad boy ways. I thought in the beginning that things may have been bad sometimes, but at least they weren't that bad. That's until I found out that the occasional weed smoking he would do was minor compared to the fact that he also added cocaine to his blunts and addicted to pills. The very first sign of abuse happened in Lincoln Courts projects in Jackson, TN. Now when I say these were the slums. I mean it seemed to me like something straight off one of those hood movies you would buy from the barber shop. Matter of fact, the day we decided to leave Kentucky to go there. As soon as we parked the car and talked to his Mom for about 15 mins there was a gang rival fight literally right in front of his Mom's house who we were moving with. He had burned all his bridges with people in Kentucky and needed a new connection so he convinced me that moving there would be good. We could stack our money and then move into our own place. Now that he was my husband, I followed suit. It was the day after I had just found out I was pregnant. His Mom had a kickback at his house and invited all their family over. The music was playing, and everyone was kicking it having a good time. I had been in the house all day, so I decided to take a shower and put some clothes on and go join the festivities.

I put my clothes on to head downstairs to talk to two of his cousins and his aunt. He was on the porch with some of his fellow Crip gang members. His cousins that I was talking to wanted me to go outside and sit with them on the porch and finish talking. So, I joined them. Mind you I had on some blue jean shorts, a gray tank top and some sandals. As soon as I stepped outside, I guess the guys were looking at me and he had seen it. He lost his mind instantly. I mean something just set him completely off. He started cursing me out and grabbed my arm and pulled me back into the house. Then told me to go upstairs and change. I cussed him back out and told him he was tripping, and I wasn't going to change. Mind you I just found out I was pregnant the day before. So, he decides that if I am not going to take the clothes off myself, he would rip them off me. So, he picks me up and packs me upstairs. Slams me on the bed and starts ripping my clothes off me until I was down to my panties and bra. I was humiliated, embarrassed, and confused because I didn't know what had caused him to go from 0 to 100 that quickly. Of course, he promised me he wouldn't do it again, blamed it on him being on the pill and that he didn't mean it so I wouldn't leave him and of course I stayed.

But from that incident led to cheating, more physical abuse, then he started accusing me of cheating. At this time, we had moved back to Bowling Green, KY. Things were only getting worse. I found myself arguing and fighting other women about this man. A man that didn't provide, protect, or even love me properly. I think about some of the things he did to me today and I ask myself how I allowed this man to have so much control over me. Growing up I'd watch movies where women were getting abused and I would always say that would never be me. Here it was me and I had no clue how to get myself out of this situation.

I had finally decided to leave him and moved back in with my Mom in Franklin, KY. I was 7 months pregnant. Completely stressed out. Here I am married, no job, my husband is running the streets, no place to live, no money, and nothing to help me with the upcoming birth of my baby girl Aviona. I had got a call that he had been arrested for driving with no license and had drugs on him. I was stressed out. I remember having a bad migraine that I tried to sleep off. My Mom had just cooked dinner so I ate and tried to lay back down thinking that would make it go away, but it didn't. I was skeptical about taking any medicine while pregnant so I told my Mom that I was going to go to the ER to see if they could just give me a shot and I would be home after that was over. I checked myself into the Emergency Room at the Medical Center of Franklin. The doctor took a urine sample and checked my vitals. When he came back, he had this look on his face. I knew something was wrong. He told me that I would not be leaving the hospital tonight and I needed to get on the phone with someone right now and have them come up here because I was about to be rushed to Bowling Green and admitted to the Medical Center of Bowling Green. My blood pressure was extremely high, and I had protein in my urine sample and that those were bad signs that my health was declining. I called my Mom and she was there within 15 mins. They gave me an IV and began pumping meds into my body rolled me on the stretcher into the ambulance and my Mom got in with me and we were on our way to Bowling Green. I was on so much medicine I don’t really remember the ride to the hospital. I remember that next day waking up in my hospital room and being told by my OBGYN Dr. Kasica that I had been diagnosed with preeclampsia/toxemia and that if I didn’t have an emergency c-section I would die from a stroke, brain damage, or have a seizure and possibly lose my life and my daughter. I had so many questions especially since I was only 7 months. It was October 6, 2007 and my daughter's due date wasn't until December 4th, 2007. I had surgery and Aviona was born and had to stay in the hospital for a month.

My husband wasn't there for the birth of his child, he was in jail. He showed up two or three days later to see my child, but my family stopped him because they knew the condition my daughter and I both were in and didn't want him to cause me stress. So, they asked the nurses to keep him away. Well that set him off, to the point that the police had to be called and he was banned from the hospital until I was healthy enough to be discharged. When Aviona finally was able to come home we didn't even have a place to stay. Didn't have time to have a baby shower or anything. But while I was in the hospital friends and family were buying things for my daughter. Aviona and I went to stay with my Mom, and he went to stay with his Dad.

The abuse continued, not only with me but now he was starting to disrespect my family. I was so conflicted. Here I am with a newborn baby and I must choose between having a relationship with my family or with my husband. By this point people were tired of me for choosing him. It had got so bad that I decided to move in with a cousin. I stayed for two days and eventually started living out of my car until I finally had enough of the abuse and checked myself and my baby into a domestic violence shelter, BRASS.

BRASS was just the peace I needed. They helped me find a job, gave me and my baby a roof over our heads, and food to eat. We stayed there for a month and they had set it up for me to be able to move into these brand-new apartments for free thanks to Section 8 with my baby. He got word and came knocking on my door every day. Begging and pleading for him to see his child and that I was wrong for keeping him away from her. The thing is I wasn't keeping her away from him. I was trying to keep him away from me. He was using our child as a pawn to get back around me. Aviona was older at this point she was about 3 or 4 months old. He had come over to bring diapers and wipes for my baby. He wasn't there for an hour. I had just fed my baby and laid her inside of her crib. I went back into the kitchen to wash the dishes and suddenly I heard 3-5 gunshots. They were coming inside our house so fast. I rushed and picked my baby up out of her crib protected her with my body as I rushed to the ground and crawled under the bed. He ran outside and started shooting back. Finally, the gunshots stopped. I get up scared to death and look at him like "What the hell is going on?" As I walk back into my daughters' room. I see two bullets right above her crib in the wall and 3 in the ceiling in the living room.

The police came but by this time he was gone. He went to retaliate without telling me what was going on. My phone instantly starts to ring. Turns out it was my cousin and a guy I knew that had done the shooting due to a prior argument that had happened earlier. I called the one person I knew that was far away from Kentucky and asked for help because I was that desperate. My Dad, he came to pick my daughter and I both up and we stayed with him for a week to relax and have peace of mind.

The day we returned I found a business card from a detective asking me to call him immediately. I called and he asked if he could come talk to me in person. I agree. He shows up with a female detective as well. They tell me that I need to tell them where my husband is now. He was involved in a string of robberies and one of them involved gunplay. All of this had occurred while we were in Mississippi. I told them I had just got back into town and that I hadn't talked to him and didn't know where he was at. That I left him and hadn't heard from him since. They seemed frustrated and acted like they didn't believe me.

They told me they would give me a few days and reach back out to me. By this time, he calls, and he is all the way in Alabama. He decides to run and is driving back and forth from Alabama, Mississippi, Tennessee, and Kentucky. The entire time he is gone. Guys from his gang are coming to my house with money, big boxes of diapers, wipes, and clothes at least two or three times a week.

I left the apartment that was shot up before they evicted me. I found a new place in Bowling Green and decided to enroll myself back into classes at WKU. Mind you when I met him, I was a sophomore in college. I was able to attend on scholarship from my grades from high school. The year he met me I had a 3.5 gpa student, active, and was having some of the best moments of my life. I withdrew a few months after we got married because I was pregnant. Dealing with someone in the streets and seeing how quick and fast the money comes in you start to get addicted to it as well. He really had me thinking that we were going to live well. That he would eventually stop being in the streets and go legit once the baby got here. That's how he got me and kept me for so long. Using his words to control my mind which was already lost and naive.

By this time the detective calls and visits started happening every day. I had been in the streets enough to know what came with this lifestyle. What to do, and what not to do. No matter what I was loyal to him and my family and nothing that I would say was going to be the reason why he did jail time. No matter what, I refused to give them any information. I refused to sign any paperwork. I think after a while they got desperate for information. Now they are threatening to charge me for things, including taking my baby away from me. At this point all I knew was that he was on the run and he wasn't coming home. Which was partially true. He went on the run from January 2008 to July 2008. Coming by to see us late at night around 2:00 am and leaving before the sun came back out. He would pay us a visit at least once a week. But he never told me where he was staying or who he was with. I begged him to turn himself in because I feared being sent to prison myself and risking my daughter being taken away from both parents. Finally, he agreed to turn himself in July 2008. He told the detectives that the only way he would turn himself in is if they stopped questioning me and not charge me with anything. My daughter was 8 months old when he turned himself in and he has been in and out of prison ever since.

My daughter is now 12 years old and I can count on both of my hands how many times she's seen him.

He caused me a different type of pain. Betrayal would some up it, but it was deeper than that. The thought of him would send me into a rage. Even seeing his face made me angry. It took me years to get over the hurt he caused me. Still till this day when I think of him, I still see myself tensing up, but I must remind myself that even through all the bullshit he caused God still gave me a beautiful blessing out of that. My daughter. Being a Mother changed me. As much as I struggled to bring her into this world, I really feel that she is my guardian angel. She was sent to protect me from myself. You see a lot of times we associate pain with hurt others have caused us, but we can also cause pain upon ourselves.

I ignored so many red flags, and when I was constantly told "I'm sorry." Instead of having a response. I should have been ok with allowing no response at all to be my response. That relationship took me from feeling worthless to showing me worth. I realized that was my biggest issue. Pointing blame. In order to fully heal I had to take accountability for my part in the situation. Why was I so comfortable allowing myself to stay in these toxic situations? Why did I put so much of who I am in the hands of a man who constantly showed me he wasn't deserving of me? Why did I care so much about how my life may look to others? Why would I prefer to look happy instead of feeling happy? This relationship taught me that we can't save everyone. A relationship should consist of two whole people. When you breakup with the person you must also break up with the pattern. This was something I didn't get until I found myself in another failed relationship with my second daughter's dad.

After divorcing in 2010, I ended up finding love again. The relationship with my now second Baby Daddy ended very badly as well. In the beginning things moved very fast. He told me he loved me first and I think the distance between us was what grew us founder. I had just moved back to Kentucky. I moved back to Kentucky and went back to college to finish my bachelor's degree after living in Nashville for 3 years. Life was good and peaceful I had been single for about a year and half before I met him. I had come into a new woman spiritually. I was Vegan, in the best shape of my life. Dating the Father of my youngest was amazing at first. We went on dates often. We were always traveling and hanging out with other couples. We had a lot of fun. Even with us living separately and in two different states. Things were going so well I trusted him, and I felt in my heart he could be the one I could spend the rest of my life with. If you would have told me then that I would be single now I wouldn't believe you. He presented himself to me as a God fearing, family-oriented man. A man who had his life together. Much different than what I was used to. He had a college degree. He worked hard. Was independent. Dressed and carried himself well, but still had a certain edge about him that I loved.

Until I found myself betrayed by him as well. The first time he betrayed me was least expected. I had drove down to his house to spend the night. He had to go to work until 11:00 that night. So, I was in his bed taking a nap. Suddenly, I hear an alarm going off. I was confused on where it was coming from because I knew it wasn't my phone. It just kept going off and it annoyed me. So, I got out of bed to search for where it was coming from. I finally hear something under his dresser. It was a phone I had never seen before. I turned the alarm off and saw that it was full of unchecked notifications. I called my number from the phone to see whose phone it was, but the phone was off. I noticed that it was connected to his Wi-Fi. So that instantly brought me suspicion.

I wasn't prepared for what I saw on that phone. Messages, texts, sexually explicit photos, videos and conversations from over 10 women. On several different apps. Conversations as current as an hour before I found the phone. I was pissed! I started crying in rage and started taking pictures on my phone of everything I saw in that phone just in case when I brought it up to him and he tried to lie I had receipts. I decided to calm down and call him. I called and said simply and calmly "Do you have anything you need to tell me?" He replied, "No. What are you talking about?" I said, "I am going to ask you something and don't you lie to me. Are you cheating on me?" He looked shocked because I had called him on Facetime. He finally lied and said "No." So I hung up and started texting him all the screenshots. He called me back and before I even let him get a word out I said "I gave you the opportunity to be truthful and you lied. So now you have two options. I can stay here until you get off and you explain to me what is going on. Or I leave right now and be done with this and block your number and you will never have to hear from me again." He said, "Please don't leave I want to talk about this."

He came to the house and gave me a bunch of excuses as men typically do when they get caught. I broke up with him and told him I wasn't going to Gatlinburg with him and his family for Christmas. I wasn't celebrating his birthday with him or anything. It was late so I didn't leave his house till that next morning. He stayed in the living room. Crying and trying repeatedly to talk to me and comfort me. I wasn't having it. I finally decide to give love another chance and the one man in the world I had faith in betrays me like this.

The next morning, I left for Kentucky. I saw a random message on my Facebook messenger from a fake page. One of the women in his phone wrote me a long message telling me how they had been talking for months prior to me. How she had a miscarriage by him. Basically, dogging him. I didn't respond. This was just adding fuel to my fire. The next few days he did everything in his power to get me to take him back. Random pop up trips to Kentucky for us to talk. Lunch dates at work. You name it. It eventually worked and I ended up in Atlanta a week later celebrating his birthday, and the week after that in Gatlinburg celebrating Christmas with him and his family.

The whole time we were in Gatlinburg I slept the whole time. I was always tired. New Year's Eve came, and we went to his cousins to celebrate. I kept falling asleep.

Something just didn't seem right. Well it ended up being that the weekend of his birthday I got pregnant. I was so mad. How could I get pregnant at a time like this? He on the other hand was very excited it was his first child.

We were still living in separate states, so he ended up surprising my daughter and I with a house. We went to our first doctor's appointment together to receive an ultrasound to see the baby. I cried like a baby. I had finally got excited. I always wanted more than one child. I hated being an only child. I never thought it would happen to me again. Especially with Aviona my oldest daughter being almost 11 years old when I found out I was pregnant. Although I was happy, I was nervous about having the same complications I had with my first child again. So was my Mom and family. I didn't want to risk losing my life again to give birth like I did with Aviona. My doctor assured me I would be ok. So, I tried to focus on the state of our relationship. We were doing good. To the world we seemed like the perfect couple. Yet secretly I was still dealing with the fact that he had cheated on me just a few months prior and I don't think I ever got over it but I didn't let it affect me because he had made positive changes to assure me he wanted us and our new family.

March 2018 my daughter and I left Kentucky and moved to Murfreesboro, TN to move into the house he had found for us. I got her enrolled in school. We got our home situated things were good. In April we found out the sex of our baby and had a gender reveal party at our house for our family and friends. Although I was bummed to be having another girl. He was super excited, and we came up with her name together. She would have his initials JGS. I thought it would be forever. I thought I had finally got over the hurt he caused and that he would be the man I knew he could be. That quickly changed again.

See when you get so caught up on love sometimes you forget to ask the important questions. Our relationship had moved so fast. A lot of things that we should have asked and found out prior to me getting pregnant and uprooting my life for him. I didn't find out until it was too late. The first few months our household ran perfectly. We split all the bills. Even prior to us living together he seemed to always be on top of things financially. Boy did that change. Money started being a big issue. I was pulling a lot more weight for someone who had a prior child and only one job. I could never understand how someone with two jobs was always late on bills.

Now mind you I was pregnant. In a city where I didn't know a soul. I was stressed out often. But nobody knew. See he was a good actor. He was one of those people who didn't post a lot on social media. Wanted people to think he was something that he wasn't. If he looked like he was doing good in front of others. He was cool. I was the complete opposite. I didn't play about my livelihood especially being a single mother for over a decade with no help. I was always on top of my finances. So, it bothered me that I seemed to be struggling more having a man than when I did when I was by myself.

He tried to pull the slack by working more but could never get himself out the hole. He was prideful and didn't want my help. Never showed me his finances so that I could help him manage them. I could never understand how he was working more and seeing me less and sacrificing the physical and emotional part of our relationship now as well. He not once put his pride to the side and fight for his family. He instead acted ungrateful. Was nonchalant about everything which made my trust shift again because I was like, "Ok you are never home because you are working. Yet we are still behind on bills. We don't go out on dates anymore. We aren't having sex. You got to be cheating again." Still till this day I believe he was cheating on me while I was pregnant. But thankfully for his sake I never found proof of that to be true. Things were growing to become worse between us.

Around July I started swelling badly. I was at work one day and told my coworker that I couldn't feel my feet anymore. At this point I couldn't wear any shoes or socks they were all too little. My job let me come to work with Crocs on because those were the only shoes I could halfway put my feet in. My coworker told me she thought I needed to call my doctor. I told her I was ok and that I would call him once I got off work. I got off, drove home and called my doctor and he told me to immediately go to the emergency room. Aviona, him, and myself drove to Nashville and I was instantly admitted. What was going on? Preeclampsia/toxemia yet again. At 7 months yet again although with Jaidyn I carried two more weeks than I did with Aviona.

I think from that moment depression started sitting in and I didn't know it. I was sad, terrified, hurt and confused. I kept asking God ``Why me?" What was so wrong with me that I could never carry a baby full term? Another pregnancy without maternity photos, without me knowing what it feels like to have real labor pains and to have my water broke. I instantly felt my pregnancy experience was robbed of me. But like most women during tough times is when we put on our strongest hat. The day I had my baby girl I literally got to see her for 30 mins. Everyone else got to go see her in the NICU as much as they wanted. I was constantly hearing other stories from people of how beautiful she was. I know they weren't doing it to be mean, but it made me sad. Did they not realize I had gone through this horrible surgery? Almost losing my life, again. To not be able to hold my baby at all. Not be able to take her home with me. I laid in the bed for eight days straight and watched everyone get to bond with my baby but me. I had listen to people tell me when and what I could do with my own child. I wouldn't wish that experience on my worst enemy and to have to sit there and watch your child fight for her life because of you. I felt like a horrible Mother even though I had no control over it.

After being in the hospital for 8 days I was finally able to go home. I am thankful that this time I did have a baby by a man who was there every step of the way for me and his child. I went to my 2 weeks check up with my doctor and I told my doctor I was feeling bad and not connected to my baby because she was still in the hospital while I was at home. Since I had another child to raise. I couldn’t go back and forth to the hospital as much as her Daddy did because he worked right next to the hospital and would stop and see her and hold her after he got off and before he came home. I didn’t know it then, but I became jealous of my own child's Father. I would cry and keep myself in the bed all day. What really set me off is knowing I was the one who had the baby but here I am going back to work before he is. I felt like my child wouldn’t even know me. She was home for only a week or two before I had to go back to work. I would cry randomly at work and one day my coworker looked at me and told me she thought I had postpartum depression. I was in denial about it for weeks. I tried to just ignore it. I was already stressed about how my kids' father was still paying bills late while working numerous jobs and on top of that recovering from labor and feeling unattached to my daughter. I finally called my nurse and told her my symptoms. She quickly asked me to come into the office and I was diagnosed with postpartum depression. I called and told my child’s father and he was so emotionless about it. He honestly acted like he didn’t care at all.

The final straw for me was one day we had got into it about our rent being 3 weeks late. I had always had my portion of the bill money. Even while on maternity leave and only making 50% of my wages. We had got into it because he was still not wanting to show me what was going on with his money and spending and still being prideful. A day before I had told him about my depression and how I felt like I missed major milestones in her life from being sick and not able to really care for her first month of her life. He had waited till I was taking a nap and took my daughter and his Mom to go get her ear pierced without Aviona and I. I was asleep and had woke up from a nap and saw that I had missed a call from him. I called him back. He didn't answer the phone. Called him back two times after that and he didn't answer the phone. I called his Mom and she didn't answer the phone. He finally called back a few hours later and had the audacity to say, "Did you call?" I said "Yeah I called. I was returning your call," He says "Well Jai and I are at Mom's. I tried to call you to see if you wanted to come watch her get her ears pierced but you didn't answer the phone." Oh, I was pissed! I said "I called you literally five minutes after you had just called me. I even called your Mom and you mean to tell me that you are just now seeing my call. On top of that you knew that's where you were going when you sat there and got her dressed to leave the house. I asked you before you left where you were going, and you told me just over your

Mom’s. So, at this point that’s a slap in the face and you did that deliberately to hurt me.”

So, I grabbed my things and my kids’ things. Packed some clothes up in the car. Go over to his Mom’s house and tell him to give me Jaidyn we were going to Kentucky. He didn’t want to give me my child. Meanwhile I am on the phone with my Mom the entire time and she’s hearing everything in the background. I asked him twice after that to give me my child. He looks at me and says “I’m not giving her to you, and you can try to take her. If you don’t like it call the police.” My Mom is in the background going off. His Mom is confused because she told me he had told her that I knew where they were going and that she didn’t know that I didn’t know they were going to get her ears pierced.

How could you allow me to tell you the issues I was struggling with? Not support me while I'm depressed. Just to kick me again while I'm down. Meanwhile I’m depressed, still making sure you had a roof over your head. Food to eat, and a clean house to come to. The police came and they told him he must give me Jaidyn because since we are not married it’s the law that the Mother has full paternity rights. He then proceeds to tell the cops “I don’t think she is even in her right mind to have my child. She is depressed." So now you want to bring up me being depressed not in a way to help and support but to kick me while I am down.

See the problem with our relationship was that he never accepted me for who I was. He accepted me for who he wanted me to be. He was fine with staying the same and not growing. While I wanted to evolve and grow. We didn't want the overall same things. One person can't be growing while the other is staying still. This situation reassured me that betrayal never comes from your enemies. Sometimes the person you would take a bullet for is the person standing behind the trigger.

Chapter 4: Loyalty

I absolutely hate this word! I hate how this generation and especially the black culture praises this word so much but fail to realize that the way we use this word is toxic to a lot of people individually and a lot of relationships. Loyalty and respect to me go hand in hand. I don't care if its family members, a spouse, or a best friend. If respect isn't given a long side loyalty, then you shouldn't give it or expect it in return._See, when it comes to dating. I had this idea in my head that if I stayed loyal and people could depend on me, then I would get the same thing in return. I realized that people are only loyal to you when they need you or can control you. Once the control and the need goes away so does the loyalty. People care so much about looking like they are loyal than being loyal. Truthfully a lot of people are only loyal to some people because they haven't been caught yet. Loyalty is about who you are and what you do when no one is around.

It took me being loyal to all the wrong people to realize how toxic this was in my life. I cared so much about being loyal to others that I refused to realize that you don't just give loyalty because you can. That you give it to people that deserve it. Never expect loyalty from dishonest people. I don't care who they are. Everyone wants loyalty but people quickly forget that you must be that person as well. I also realized that I would use the fact that I was a loyal person to try to control a lot of situations. Making myself look better because even though a person could do me dirty many times. At least I could say that I didn't. So that would be my gateway to keep people where I wanted them to be and to make them feel bad without them even knowing that's what I was doing. It was my way of getting back without doing people how they did me. Which is toxic. I see it happening all the time especially with black people and especially black women. Stop allowing the unworthy to determine your worth. Decide what you deserve and don't settle until you get exactly that.

November 10, 2010 the day my divorce was finalized. It's crazy that when I got married it literally took 10 mins, but to divorce took about 6 months even with him being in prison. After staying married to him and holding him down 2 and half years straight from prison. I woke up one day and I was just done with everything. I no longer had the desire to stay in a relationship just because I wanted my family. Everything left. My attraction to him, I mean everything. After months of trying to get through to him that I wasn't willing to stay in this marriage anymore. He finally decided to apply for divorce papers in jail. I went online and read that if an inmate in prison applies for a divorce while incarcerated the divorce would be free. He finally agreed and since he didn't have anything that I wanted. The judge granted me full custody of my daughter, my maiden name back, and my singleness. The only three things I asked for and the only three things I wanted. It took a few months after my divorce to get used to it. While most people my age were partying and enjoying life. I had grown up so fast that I had to think about how I was going to provide for my child. Especially knowing that my ex still had 5 more years to do in prison before he would get out.

What was I going to do? I had quit college. I had no real job experience. Only thing I had was government assistance. So, I decided to go back to school and work part time in a clothing store. I did that for a few months, but it just wasn't enough. I needed a side hustle and fast. During this season of my life I didn't realize that I should have just been focused on trying to heal. Instead I went straight to survival mode. All while neglecting my healing process. Fighting my demons and truly evaluating what I had just gone through. So, by doing that I caused myself to go from one bad situation to another. Except this time, it wasn't a relationship. I was single for the first time in my adult life. Now at 22 years old. I had been married, a new Mom, homeless, and now divorced and very broke. Until one day at school I got approached by a classmate from Louisville. He had told me that he was thinking about stepping into the party promoting business and wanted to see if I could help him get people to come since I was from the area and he wasn't. That in return he would pay me to help promote. Sounded easy enough to me and Dre was someone I considered a friend so of course I jumped on the opportunity. This is a way I could help a friend and put money in my pocket.

The first party was at this place called You & Me in Bowling Green and when I say it was a flop. It was a flop. Nobody showed up but the girls I had invited out. So of course, I didn't get paid for it. So, my friend went back to the drawing board and decided that the best way to get people to show up is by having a better party flyer and a better social media preference. So, he had me get a group of girls around campus and hire them as official brand ambassadors for his now new party promoting business named IPayME Productions. Well I think he got too nervous to have more events in Bowling Green so the girls I had gathered never got a chance to work, but he told me he was thinking of doing something in Louisville on a Friday night and he wanted me to host it.

Now mind you I had only been to Louisville twice before and I wasn't too familiar with going to big cities. Louisville was a big city to me coming from a small country town like Franklin. I agreed and just continued working and going to class until the day of the event because it was a few weeks away. While I was waiting to work the party in Louisville I randomly out of the blue got approached by a photographer from Lexington, KY. He told me that he had seen a picture of me from someone's page and thought I had a good face for modeling. I thought at first this man had to be joking right. I asked him if he meant to send that message to me. He laughed and said "Yes, I did." and asked me if I had ever considered modeling. I said no, never been something I have been passionate about. He then goes to ask me if I would be interested in taking some pictures for him and he would come to Bowling Green and do them for free. I was like well this couldn't be that hard. So, I agreed and got my friend Charles to help style me. I didn't have a makeup artist, didn't get my hair done. It was just me, the clothes Charles had picked for me to wear and the places we found in Bowling Green to shoot. We took every photo outside. At first, I was so lost and confused. I asked the photographer "What do you want me to do just smile?" I had no clue what I was doing out there. I gave myself a pep talk and thought to myself "As many pictures as you took in high school and before you go to the club you got more confidence than this now Kendra." So, it was one pose he had me do. I had on a burnt orange dress with some stockings and some heels and my hair was shaved on the left side and long on the right side. I slanted my legs in like how I had seen the girls do on "America's Next Top Model" and my friend and photographer asked me to do it in the middle of the street. From then I changed into this black one-piece lingerie outfit and we took some pictures while it was dark outside in a field. I remember getting ate up by mosquitos bad. I did it and we finished up the shoot and I went home. He told me that he was going to edit the best pictures and send them to me in a few days.

A few days passed and I started getting all kinds of notifications on Facebook. He had posted the picture of me in the street to his page and people loved it. I had really good feedback. Then the next day he posted a pic of me in the lingerie and my notifications really went crazy. Well Dre, my friend I was promoting parties with, saw that and was like "That's it. That's how we are going to get this money. I am going to get you to do another shoot and I am going to use your photos for the flyer and that's how we are going to get people to come out." Well, that's exactly what he did. From there, I began to become very popular in Louisville. I would go to school and drive to Louisville and have a party and drive back that same night and be at school the next day at 8:00 am I did that every week straight for about 3 months.

Until I started getting approached by photographers in Atlanta, and Nashville. Nashville became like a second home to me. One photographer in general is the photographer I did most of my published work with. Tavell Brown of Brown Photograph, or as I always call him Velly Bear. This man is responsible for the photos you saw in Straight Stuntin Magazine. He always had my back. Lord knows I got on this man's nerves with all my crazy ideas. I was hardheaded and I never listened to anything he said. I always had a million questions and wanted to do things my way. I loved working with him at his studio. He was always professional and made me comfortable. Once I reached a certain level publications reached out to me instead of me having to chase jobs. I had such a good relationship with Tavell that I would request that I take my pictures with him and not their in-house photographers. Although I worked with other photographers in other cities like Chicago, Louisville, Lexington, Miami, and Atlanta. He is and will always be my favorite. These photographers hadn't worked with many girls from Kentucky. I was the first model to be published in some of these national magazines from Kentucky. I worked hard to achieve that. So hard that I ended up getting to do music videos, gracing the covers of magazines, traveling the world, being on the radio, and working at BET Hip Hop Awards. I even dated a few celebrities. Mostly rappers. I was single, making money, and seeing the world something I was not used to at all. Plus, the attention I was getting from it was exactly what I thought I needed in order to feel confident and sexy again.

I went from being married to a man who would get mad if another man looked at me. Cheated on me constantly. Always telling me I wouldn't be nothing without him and nobody was going to want me because I had a baby. To being desired from men all over the world. Oh, couldn't nobody tell me nothing! I was dating rappers who would give me anything I wanted. Going into parties for free and not having to stand in line. Even having my own security, my own hotel to stay at before and after the party, being paid to party twice a week. Free food, free liquor, I was living the life. Or at least I thought I was. Here I am reassuring myself that what I am doing is ok because I'm making money to provide for my child. I started losing friends. I started hearing rumors that I was a stripper, a porn star, a hoe, a prostitute you name it I was called it. I was being told that people thought I had reached the level of success I had reached because I was sleeping with photographers to get the gigs. I would go back and forth online trying to defend myself. I even got into a few physical altercations with some females about it. Until one day I just got tired of doing that and started not to care what people thought or said about me. In my mind, opinions of others weren't helping me pay bills or take care of my daughter. That was the first time in my life that I didn't care what other opinions of me were and I loved every bit of it.

Meanwhile, deep inside I was so unhappy, broke as hell, the money was coming and going as quickly as I was making it. I was popular and loved by so many people but on the inside, I was depressed and really didn't want to be doing what I was doing. Believe it or not modeling was the hardest I had ever worked for something. I took it very seriously. As many times as I would go on set and see girls exploit themselves. I just didn't have that in me. I remember one time I got booked to do a photoshoot in Miami and to act in a short film about a hood love story. The promoter who booked me was from Chicago and he took me out to the strip club with him, his girlfriend and his homeboy. The minute I stepped foot in that club men and women were trying to ask me to meet up with them after the party was over to hang out. My dumb naive self was going to do it thinking they just wanted to party some more. Well good thing the promoter I was with overheard the conversation and he begged me not to go. I was like why not. He said, “Girl they are going to try to pimp you to work at this club or have you working the streets.” From that day on I knew what kind of lifestyle I had got myself into.

All I was to these people was another pretty face with a nice body, disposable. That made me go even harder because now I had to prove a point that not all models had to strip or sell ass to be successful and that’s exactly what I did. That trip in Miami, I had done a photoshoot at the same location and with same photographer as a famous stripper who is now a rapper, and reality tv star from Love and Hip-Hop Atlanta. She was finishing her shoot while I was getting my makeup prepared for mine. We had a casual conversation about life and the industry we were in. She told me some of the things she had done but told me if it wasn’t for stripping, she would be broke because modeling really wasn’t making her any money. She got her name from being a well-known exotic dancer. We laughed as we talked about some of the celebrities that would slide in our DM's. Only to find out that we had some common men in our messages.

I left that trip with a lot on my mind. Something in my spirit just didn't feel right. I instantly started feeling a strong sense of guilt. I started to think about how what I was doing was affecting the people that mattered to me the most. My daughter and my Mom. I started thinking about all the things that were so available to me online and thinking that one day my child would be old enough to go online and see her Mom dressed half naked. I remember crying and staying in bed all day. I didn't eat, I didn't pick up the phone and talk to anybody. I just prayed and asked God to show me where I needed to go. I wasn't happy. I was tired and I wanted better for my child and myself.

The week before I went to Miami, I had received 2 of my biggest modeling gigs ever. I had also started to get a little serious with a well-known Atlanta rapper. One of the gigs was the cover and spread of a magazine called Vixens Magazine and the other was a casting for a few scenes on Love and Hip-Hop Atlanta. I had wanted to get into the acting world, and this was finally my chance. But after my meltdown I decided to quit. I had already completed the cover of the magazine and I decided to make that the last thing that I ever did in this industry. I reached out to the casting director for Love and Hip Hop and told them that I had to decline. I got my number changed and cut things off with the rapper. That was in 2012 and I never went back, and it was probably the best decision I could have ever made.

I often get asked “Why did you quit at such a high peak of your career?” Even today I am still asked to take pictures, promote events, and model in music videos. At the end of the day. I just felt like I was at a point in my life that anything I associate my name with must be good for my soul. It must be something I want my daughters to be proud of. Do I regret the choices I made? Absolutely not because it’s a part of my story. If I could speak to any young lady out there right now who thinks this life is to have. I would tell her to really think about the real reason she is wanting to do it. Think if those reasons have any real substance to the growth and direction of your life and your overall goals. If not, don’t do it. I made the decision to model during a time where I was desperate, lacked confidence in myself, and really thought that was my only option.

See, during this time I was so busy being loyal to others. That I wasn't being loyal to myself. Which made me put myself in situations I would eventually try to justify. When deep down inside. My intuition always told me it was wrong. Struggle can make you do things you thought you would never do. One thing I learned from that situation is to always be loyal to your own peace of mind first and foremost.

Chapter 5: Manipulation

Some people are truly great with making you feel like you are the problem. Narcissists only surround themselves with people they feel they can’t get over. Anyone else with an opinion that differs from theirs are usually people they don’t surround themselves with very long. After being single for a few years now after my divorce. I found myself dealing with narcissists, after narcissists. One I ended up engaged to but thank God we didn’t end up having any kids or getting married. This man asked me to marry him, let me plan a wedding, and then tell me he didn’t want to go through it anymore. Only to find out it was because he had been cheating.

I left that failed relationship and about 2 years later ended up with the Father of my second daughter Jaidyn. I am naturally a healer. So unknowingly broken people tend to cling to me. In every relationship I have been in. I have always been the one to have to sacrifice the most. Whether it be my dreams, my comfort, my stability, my hobbies, whatever it was. I was always willing to stop everything to make the relationship work. It wasn’t until my last relationship that I learned I had a thing for falling for Narcissists or manipulators. You see narcissists are people that can't be fixed because they don’t want to be fixed.

They have the mindset that allows them to abuse others while still believing they are the victims.

What they do to get you they don’t do to keep you. I hate when people say, “Well you picked your kids Father or Mother.” This is true but people fail to realize that people change. Most of the times you don’t see the change until it’s too late because you’re too caught up being in love. Therefore, I feel like I have never really been in love. I have only had strong infatuation or loved a version of them I saw within them based off the potential I felt they had. When I should have focused on what I was seeing in the present. Observed and allowed the man to be just as vulnerable as me from the beginning. Instead of being so quick to put myself out there.

You can’t save everyone. Everyone’s issues aren't yours to fix. The worse manipulation ever is meeting a man and they at first want to know everything about you. They want to learn what you like and what you dislike. Do it to make you fall. Then do everything they said they wouldn’t do and hurt you. Of course, it’s good to be with someone who has the same vision as you. I know from my experiences with bad relationships that as you grow older your interest and wants change. So, it's important to have someone who is willing to accept the growth with you. I've never had that. Instead I let the fear of being alone cause me to make the wrong decisions and to fall for men whose only intention was to manipulate their way into my life. To be more focused on showing me off then really loving me.

See weak people can't deal with strong people. People who cause them to be uncomfortable. My last relationship I was manipulated badly. So bad that I was told after I had already caught feelings for him that although him and his ex-wife hadn't been together for two plus years. That he was still legally married to her. He was good at manipulating. That he even had his family thinking he was divorced. There wasn't anything that he could tell me that I didn't believe because we were spending so much time together. He didn't do anything without me, or at least that was what it seemed like. I thought I fell in love with a man who still till this day isn't the man I met. It's crazy because my youngest child's Father and I despite how much everyone thought we were going to marry and live happily ever after are the most incompatible people ever. He eventually got divorced a few months after I found out I was pregnant. Gratefully, we get along fine now and co parent wonderfully together. But sometimes people just aren't for you and we were not made for one another, and that's fine. Sometimes things fall apart so that better things can form.

Being manipulated can have a huge effect on your growth and finding your purpose. For me I noticed that I would get depressed and have bad anxiety because I would always find myself putting other people's needs before mine. It completely ruined my trust with men. I don't put nothing past anyone but especially a man. I also realized that with being an only child I was even manipulated by my parents. I always felt like it was wrong for me to love both parents. That I had to pick a side. Which eventually made me shut down and hold back certain information and discussions with them because I was afraid one would get jealous of the other.

The only way for me to cope was to completely disengage myself. I had to be ok with loving people from a distance. Whether it be family, friends, coworkers, or a spouse. Loving myself more than I loved another. Taking time out to get back to doing the things that I wanted to. I went back to school. I started a business and wrote this book. I traveled more, got back to being healthy and working out. Just falling in love with myself again. I now know why single people stay single for so long. Once you heal from difficult things that people have done to you by yourself and without an apology. The peace that comes in your life is something you don't want to risk again.

I am careful about the people I interact with now. If you can't positively affect my life, I don't want you around. If I can't gain from you just as much as you can gain from me the relationship is irrelevant to me. It's perfectly ok to be selfish with yourself. Falling in love with yourself is the first ingredient to happiness and purpose. Beware of things that make your heart feel a certain way so quickly. Love is patient and love is kind. They could just be manipulating your heart because they don't know how to control their own.

Chapter 6: Grief

Death is something we will all experience. Mourning a loss is something nobody does the same. We all have lost loved ones but sometimes you lose people that you will never truly get over. In my lifetime. I have lost both of my biological Grandfathers. I never got to meet my Mom's or my Dad's real fathers. My Mom's Dad died while she was a baby. My Dad's Father never claimed him. So, I was never got to meet him. The crazy part about this is when he did pass away. My Father was asked to do his eulogy at his funeral, and he did it.

The two toughest deaths I have ever had to experience were the loss of my Stepdad Hoss and the loss of my first love and high school sweetheart Kennard. In 2017 is when Kennard left this world way too early. He was a father, a son, a brother, and friend to many people. So many people loved this man and took it hard when he left us. I will never forget the phone call I got. I was at work and my Mom called and said, "Kendra have you heard about your friend he has been shot." I sat there for a second and then I replied "Huh?" Mom then goes to say, "Yes he got shot in Franklin and he is in the hospital."

I immediately got up from my desk and walked outside and sat on the bench. Something in my gut knew something was wrong but I just knew he would pull through. Then five minutes later my phone starts blowing up. I start getting calls from everyone asking me if I am ok because he didn't make it.

We met in the 9th grade. We got introduced by my best friend Kesha. I was told that he would stop by their house often to kickback and clown because his cousin lived next door. If you knew him, you knew that was all he did was laugh. One day he saw a picture of me and kept asking them who I was. Till finally he asked my best friend for my number. Kesha told him she wasn't giving him my number because I didn't know him, and she wasn't just going to be passing my number out like that. So, he said "Well call her so I can talk to her." Kesha called me that night and said, "Girl this boy wants to talk to you." I said, "Girl what boy?" She said, "He has been asking for your number, but I told him I wasn't giving it to him."

He gets on the phone and I could tell he was nervous or shy. He asked me a few questions and we conversed until he finally asked me for my number. I told him to put Kesha back on the phone first. Kesha gets on the phone and I say “Girl should I give him my number. Is he cute?” Kesha says “Yea he isn’t ugly. He has braids and he is brown skinned and from Russellville. I mean he is cool. Y'all should talk.” So, I agreed and gave him my number and we were dating soon after that.

He was so funny and the opposite of me. He was daring and spontaneous. While I was calculated and strategic. We didn’t live in the same town which made it difficult as high schoolers. Our focus was on two different things at the time. But no matter how many times we started and ended things. We always stayed in touch because if we didn’t have anything else, we had a real friendship. We always had the ability to pick up exactly where we left

I went on to get married and have my first child. Around that time, he had a bad motorcycle accident. I didn't have his number anymore, so I sent him a message to his Facebook page. Once he got out and was better. He told me he appreciated me reaching out, but he was upset with me. He felt I had got married too soon and didn’t like the things he was hearing about my then husband and how he was treating me. We had the kind of relationship that we could be honest about how we felt for one another but respect one another and allow ourselves to just be friends. I think we truly wanted each other to be happy even if that meant not together.

I didn't hear from him after that. He unfortunately had to do some time away in prison time. Around the same time my husband was going on his second year in prison and we ended up divorcing. While he was locked up, he reached out to a mutual friend of ours and told her he was being moved to a halfway house and he wanted to reach out to me and see what I was up to. That next week I received a card, a letter, and a picture in the mail from him. I still have it till this day. From that day we were on the phone every day. I was driving to Louisville to see him and it was like we hadn't stopped talking at all.

He loved music even though he never knew the words to the songs. He would call me late at night and just play songs over the phone singing them loudly in my ear. Any new song that came out he always wanted to know what my opinion of it was. He knew I was really into music. We often would talk about all the crazy things we did in high school. Over time I grew very fond of his family, but especially his Dad. I always called him Pops. I love that man like he is my own Father and will always feel strongly about him.

Once he was released from jail. I had started modeling and traveling so I was never in town. He and I both had our first kid by now. We tried to date again but I always respected our friendship more than anything. We were both hustlers and always on the move. So, we decided to go our separate ways in 2010 for good. From 2010 until 2017 we would check on one another periodically and especially on our birthdays. He is the one person that I can say that I dated that knew the real me. I could be myself around him and he accepted me for who I was always. We didn't try to change one another. We accepted each other and that's something I always loved and respected him for.

It had been about a year or so since I had heard from him. May 29th I randomly get a Snapchat message from him. I still have the message saved on my phone. It's a video of him singing in the shower to me. I messaged him back and said, "You still can't learn the words to songs I see." He said "Hell Naw!" He proceeds to say something else that I will keep with me forever. I don't want to share and haven't shared it with anyone. I feel in my heart God told him to do that so that I would always know how much he cared about me. Two days later, May 31st to be exact he passed away.

I cried for days at a time. I didn't get out of the bed. I didn't talk to anyone. I truly believe in my heart God wanted him to reach out to me those few days before. I couldn't make myself go to the funeral. I wanted my final moment seeing him to be more private and intimate, not rushed or around a lot of people. I decided just to go to his visitation and my best friend Kesha went with me. I remember walking in and seeing two of the Mothers of his children. I said hello to them and gave them my condolences. They must be some of the strongest women I ever met. I will always have nothing but respect for them. I couldn't imagine how they or any of the other Mothers of his children felt and go through even now. I remember speaking to one of his kids Mom's a few days before his funeral. I had messaged her to tell her that I was praying for her. Just to let her know that I was genuinely thinking of her and her baby. She ended up bringing comfort to me without even knowing it. She solidified to me the exact same thing he had just told me days before he passed.

I couldn't even look at him. One glance and I was a complete mess. I went over to his Dad and I hugged him so tight. I am sure I made his shirt wet from my tears, but as he has always been able to do. He knew exactly what to say to calm me down and comfort me.

One of the biggest things that makes it so hard for me to deal with is because he lost his life in my hometown. That still doesn't sit well with me. I never really felt like I got to grieve properly due to several reasons. One being social media and people and their uncalled-for opinions and assumptions. Secondly because it was in my hometown. Around people I know he thought was his friend and still nobody is held accountable. It wasn't until the spring of 2019 that I even went to visit his gravesite. That was when it became final for me. I was able to say my goodbyes in peace. I remember cleaning around his beautiful head stone. Making sure everything looked nice before I left. It was such a pretty day outside that day. I just sat and talked to him like he was right in front of my face. I miss him so much. He should be here. Certain songs I hear remind me of him. When I go home to visit my Mom. I still have all the pictures and letters from him that date back to high school. Losing him was so painful but I can say that one thing he and his situation taught me is to not take life for granted. Live everyday like it's your last. Don't live in fear. Work hard but play hard just as much. See the world.

Create experiences and memories. Don't sweat the small stuff. Be more appreciative of life and value your time.

March 4, 2019 was the last day I laid eyes on the only man I consider a Father. Hoss came into my life at an early age and is still till this day the only man my Mom trusted enough to really bring around me. Although they never got married and had broken up long before he passed away. I will always consider him my Stepdad. This man coming into my life was one of my greatest and happiest childhood memories. I was a little girl when I met him. I don't even think I was in the first grade. Hoss was just so cool to me. People today always ask me where my love for UofL and Celtics basketball came from and I have always said it came from him. I remember being a little girl and watching Larry Bird play on tv. Hoss loved how Larry Bird played the game. I eventually began to love it too and to love the entire organization. Hoss always had Louisville basketball memorabilia in his car or around the house. He loved Cardinal red and was one of the most loyal fans I have ever known.

Before he got sick, he worked for a local furniture store. Sometimes he would take me with him, and I loved riding in the truck with him to jobs. Especially when we had to go out of town because I knew we would always stop by one of two places for breakfast. The donut shop right down the street from Friendly Furniture or Hardees. His spirit was the thing I loved most about him. From my memory he always respected my Mom and my biological Dad. In fact, still to this day my Father speaks highly of Hoss because he never overstepped his boundaries. He wasn't one of those men who did too much to make you like him. He was genuine. He never asked me to call him Dad, but I know in his heart that he knew I always saw him as a Father and not just my Mom's boyfriend. I don't think I ever saw him in a bad mood because he was always somewhere laughing. His laugh was very distinctive. Not a laugh in this world can compare if you ever heard it you instantly knew it was him.

There is a picture of me as a little girl sitting on top of his long mustard yellow Cadillac. Hoss was a smooth man and he didn't play about his car. He would go outside and clean that car all the time. So much I think it used to get on my Mom's nerves. On summer days he always kept his straw hat in the car. He was always working. Always enjoyed laughing. Always smiling. I don't think I ever heard him raise his voice, complain, or worry. Then one day we got the call he had a stroke and was in the hospital.

I remember him declining quickly because he went from the hospital, to a rehabilitation center, and finally to a nursing home. He would spend 20 plus years of his life sick. During that time my Mom and him split up. Once I become an adult. I would go visit him at the nursing home. I even took my daughter Aviona to go meet him and every time I came, he was always smiling. He never forgot who I was, and he always asked me about my Mom. He would always tell me that he loved me and was proud of me.

The day he was buried I cried. I cried hard. I had felt so sad because he didn't get to live out his full life because he was sick. I was wondering how my life would have turned out had he not got sick and was still with my Mom. It took me going to visit him shortly after he was buried. That it resonated with me that not one day did this man feel sorry for himself. He made every day of his life full of laughter and happiness. Even while sick and wheelchair bound. He still never complained. He was a man of such courage and humility. I will always admire him for that, and I miss him deeply. I hate my youngest daughter Jaidyn won't get to meet him.

Grief forces you to see who matters. Who never did matter? Who won't anymore and who always did? I don't think grief gets easier. I think you learn to cope with it after a while. Grief is a powerful way to help you find your purpose. It also comes with a steep price. It also teaches us not to take life and time for granted. Cherish every moment. Make memories. Live life. Be fearless. Be present.

Chapter 7: Accountability

Out of everything I experienced in life. Being accountable for my own actions has been the best thing to really force me to grow and that's been productive to my evolution. See it's easy to play victim. It's easy to point blame, but it's hard to recognize your own faults and failures. I really feel that taking the time to love myself helped me to get to this point of my life. Being single this time really forced me to DO THE WORK! I realized that I have experienced every aspect of a relationship and I'm only 32 years old. I've been engaged (more than once), married, gave birth to children within a marriage and not married, divorced, and even had an ex die. So many failed relationships and even childhood trauma. Patterns I am sure I repeated not knowingly because sometimes we focus so much on what a person done to us that we fail to take the time to see what we allowed them to do.

So, last year forced me to "DO THE WORK". I realized that every failed relationship was because of me just as much as it was because of someone else. I had to really take accountability for my own actions. I learned the nasty, dirty truth about myself. I learned that I don't know how to be happy and can't function in peace because I am used to toxicity, dysfunction, and chaos. So much to the point that I'll self-sabotage the relationship because I am uncomfortable with healthy relationships. So uncomfortable that I may run back to what's familiar. I learned that I can be manipulative especially when things aren't going my way. I will try to make a person feel bad for not feeling how I feel and not giving me what I want. I learned that I forgive and don't forget so at any given time I'll rehash past arguments to prove a point and make myself seem right. I learned that I'm a control freak. Being so used to doing things on my own. I don't know how to accept help or even ask. I learned that I am passive aggressive. That I like to hurt people with my words and not my actions. That I move too fast and stay too long. That I have a habit of falling for men who need me more than want me. That I'm ok with accepting people's flaws and I fall for potential they don't even see themselves. That I'm ok with accepting multiple red flags instead of realizing that it's ok to leave once I spot one. That I have self-worth issues. I am very insecure and fear being alone. That I would associate being alone with not being wanted. Which I learned triggered from childhood trauma of not having an active Father.

The hardest thing I've learned is that people can only love you how they can love you. We all have our own love language. How you give and receive love can be totally translated a different way to someone else. We must be ok with that and be ok with meeting people where they are. To be accountable means to grow. How can you ever improve in life if you are never wrong? I wasted so many years blaming the failure of my life on everyone who did me wrong. It was all their fault and not mine. Until one day I realized I have a few toxic traits myself. See it's easy to throw rocks and hide your hand. It's easy to see other people's faults before you see your own. To truly grow into your full potential, you must be willing to be real and raw with yourself.

On my personal journey I had to realize that you play a major role in every good and bad thing that happens to your life. You can pray until your knees are sore. You can ask and receive advice from others. But at the end of the day most of us are always going to do what we want anyway. If you choose to suffer you will suffer. If you choose to be unhappy you will. Accountability is important in every role of your life. Business, finances, health, relationships, and mentality. It is also beneficial to have people in your life that can help you be accountable as well. You never want people around you who won't tell you the truth even when it hurts and not even asked for. Sometimes the reason we can't be accountable is because we put too much power in words, people, noise, and other distractions. Most of us self-sabotage our own lives. Most of us don't take the time to heal our own wounds before spreading that pain onto someone else who is also broken.

Be real with where you are in life. Be real with your issues. Seek counseling if you need to because sometimes, we experience things that we think aren't affecting us, but the hurt comes out in other ways and in other situations. For example, with me my childhood trauma with men bleed into my relationships with men. I would give men more power and control over my life than they deserved. I was ok with giving everything with little expectations. I am not perfect. I too have also been controlling due to my fear and lack of trust. We all have things we go through and must deal with. It takes time and effort. Be realistic and be patient in the healing process. Accountably isn't only what we do. It is also what we chose not to do.

Chapter 8: Forgiveness

Everything in life is forgivable. Yes, you read that right. I truly feel that way. Honestly, I feel that because I chose not to hold grudges is the reason why God blesses me the way that He does. I truly feel that without forgiveness you will not reach the levels of life nor your purpose. There is no love without forgiveness. I like to think that people deserve the same grace and mercy that we want God to give us. Holding grudges never affects the person who does the harm more than it will affect you. As the saying goes. 'I can forgive but I can't forget." Not forgetting is completely fine. The problem with that and how it could potentially affect your growth and enable you from reaching your full potential is because it could eventually lead you into "keeping score" is what I like to call it. You will begin waiting and preparing yourself to get hurt just so you can say "I told you so." or "I knew I shouldn't have forgave you."

It wasn't until a few months before I published this book that I had to put my own forgiveness struggles to test. The one person on earth I had always had trouble forgiving was my Dad. As I began writing this book, I knew that I would eventually have to sit down and have a conversation with both of my parents. I didn't want to blindside the two people I love most in this world. I also didn't want my Dad to feel that telling my truth was coming from a malicious standpoint. I try not to use my words to hurt people anymore. So, I didn't want him to be hurt by anything I said. Nor did I want him to find out things about me from a book instead of out my mouth. I had struggled for months on how to tell him about it because let's be honest. Our communication has never been consistent. So, I just prayed and asked God to reveal the best time for us to have this conversation.

One day out of the blue my Dad called me. I could tell in his voice that this wasn't going to be one of those five-minute calls just to check on my daughters and me. I could feel the conviction in his voice. We finally had the conversation I have been wanting to have with him for 32 years. My Dad has always told me how much he was sorry for not being there and how much he loved me. Honestly never really believed him. The conversations would always end with him pointing blame and not taking full accountability of his own actions. To finally hear my Dad, say the things I have been waiting for him to say and to also be completely honest and up front with him about how I felt, took a load off my shoulders.

I also wondered how I would feel after this conversation. I wondered if after I told him how I really felt about him would he still reach out. Or would he be distant? The conversation surprisingly went very well. My Dad respected me and my point of view and finally listened to understand and not to respond. I forgave him but I was truthful and told him it would be a work in progress. We have been reaching out to each other more than usual, so things are going well. He even has been calling to invite me to things at his house.

I think the fact that I have been able to also forgive the Fathers of my kids says a lot on how I have allowed my pain to fuel my purpose. After all the resentment I had built up. It says a lot about where I am now versus a few years ago. I think once you can forgive and forget you get your power back. You can take all that negative energy and use it to source more positive things in your life. Sometimes you just must be done. You can't change people. You can change the people you want around you and what you accept from them.

It is only when you can forgive that you can really begin to live in peace. It's draining staying mad. I had to learn to forgive others even when they don't deserve it. It's not for them, it is always for you. It doesn't make you weak or stupid it makes you the bravest and the strongest. It's not always easy and it can be painful. Everyone makes mistakes. If you can't forgive others, then why should you expect someone to forgive you. Most of the time you spend holding a grudge for a person. That person has moved on with their life. Holding grudges makes you toxic and bitter. I try to always remember forgiving is healing, and where you are healing you are growing.

Conclusion:

Pressure builds diamonds. Our journey in life will never be the same. Throughout my life I have had many struggles and even though I spoke on a lot of those in this book it is still a lot I did not share. Every chapter in this book entails an emotion I feel has personally got me to the point in my life where I feel I know what my purpose is. A teacher I once had in college told me "Once you find out the meaning God put you on this earth you have mastered living." To me it took me experiencing everything that was set up to destroy me for me to realize my real purpose in life is to simply be happy. To be an authentic person in a world that seeks perfection. To use my strength to be voice for people who don't have the strength to speak for themselves. Sounds simple but you will be surprised how many people stay silent, complacent, compromise and settle out of fear and never really experience a full and happy life. To me your purpose is whatever your passion is and whatever comes natural to you. Since I was a little girl. I have always been outspoken and willing to say things others weren't. To stand for what I thought was right. My passion in life is helping others. Once you know your passion you know your purpose.

Since writing this book I have grown. If there is anyone reading this and struggling with being single. Remember that when you are single is the time that you should be the most focused on bettering yourself. Do not allow yourself to get into a relationship when you don't have yourself together. You never want to be a project. Make the most out of singleness. Time is valuable and precious. Don't take it for granted. Live your life. Travel, or start a business, and get healthy. The time you invest into yourself is the most valuable and you will appreciate it so much. When the time comes for you to experience love again you will be in a happier place because you are happy with yourself. You don't find the perfect relationship you build it and building it will always be easier when both parties are whole and healed.

Some things change and some things stay the same. I am so happy that my ex (my youngest daughters Dad) and I are co-parenting well. I must admit he is an amazing Father and a great help to me. It turned out that not being together ended up being the best thing for us. As far as my ex-husband is concerned, we will probably never be friends and I am completely ok with that. Once I lose respect for a person it's pretty much no going back for me. I wish him well and pray he finds himself sooner than later. My Father and I are still communicating so that is good. Could it be better? Yes! Are there still gaps? Yes! I've learned to accept things for what they are and be ok with the things I cannot change.

I have decided that while I am living and loving my life. Walking in my purpose every day that I must live to understand myself and never to be understood. I trust that God will place and remove the right and wrong people in my life. A closed door isn't the end but could end up being a blessing. I no longer have the energy to feel like I must cut people off because I learned in my last relationship. If you're growing the ones that aren't for you will eventually cut themselves off. I still don't have a heart that sets out to be revengeful. God has never failed me yet and anything a person has done wrong to me. He has had the last word. Like the bible says, "vengeance is not mine, it's the Lord's."

I've learned that it's ok to be a complete hot mess. It's ok not to be ok and not have the answers. It's never ok to neglect your feelings for the sake of others. Self-love is the best love. Loyalty is rare, be very careful who you give it to. I wasted many years thinking I was riding and dying when all I was doing was dying. The people you keep around you are also important in your journey. Get you some real friends who will hold you accountable. Inspire you. Pray with and for you. Who accepts you and loves you at your authentic self. A person who doesn't have the same mentality as you shouldn't be around you. Likeminded people is crucial.

To all the young ladies who will read this remember that your body is made for love and not play. Respect yourself always and realize just how precious and powerful you are. When a woman understands her purpose, she can't be pursued by just anybody. His pursuit must be familiar with the one who created him. Don't rush. Trust the process always. Life's greatest lessons are always revealed at the worst times. So be ok with making mistakes. Pain makes you stronger. Betrayal makes you wiser. Loyalty should be earned. Manipulation is not love. Grief has no expiration date. Accountability is a sign of maturity. Forgiveness is power and the final form of love. Your problems nor your past are ever greater than your purpose.

www.ingramcontent.com/pod-product-compliance
Ingram Content Group UK Ltd.
Pitfield, Milton Keynes, MK11 3LW, UK
UKHW041925190726
13854UKWH00003B/1444

9 780578 654072